CLIMATE CHANGE

Sally Morgan

FRANKLIN WATTS
LONDON • SYDNEY

First published in 2007 by
Franklin Watts
338 Euston Road, London NW1 3BH

Franklin Watts Australia
Level 17/207 Kent Street, Sydney, NSW 2000

EARTH SOS is based on the series EarthWatch published by Franklin Watts.
It was produced for Franklin Watts by Bender Richardson White,
P O Box 266, Uxbridge UB9 5NX.
Project Editor: Lionel Bender
Text Editor: Jenny Vaughan
Original text adapted and updated by: Jenny Vaughan
Designer: Ben White
Picture Researchers: Cathy Stastny and Daniela Marceddu
Media Conversion and Make-up: Mike Weintroub,
          MW Graphics, and Clare Oliver
Production: Kim Richardson

For Franklin Watts:
Series Editor: Melanie Palmer
Art Director: Jonathan Hair
Cover Design: Chi Leung

A CIP catalogue record for this book is available from the British Library.

Dewey classification 363.738'74

ISBN 978 0 7496 7670 4

Printed in China

Picture Credits: Oxford Scientific Films: cover main photo & pages 22-23
top (Richard Packwood), cover small photo & pages 6 (Daniel J. Cox), 5
top (Martyn Chillmaid), 13 top (Michael Fogden), 19 top (Edward
Parker), 20-21 (Kim Westerskov), 27 bottom (William Paton/Survival
Anglia). The Stock Market Photo Agency Inc.: cover globe & pages 1, 6-
7, 9, 11 bottom, 16, 18, 22-23 (J. M. Roberts), 24. Science Photo Library,
London: pages 4 (Alex Bartel), 8 (European Space Agency), 12, 14 (John
Eastcott & Yva Momatiuk), 17 top (Hank Morgan), 17 bottom (Carlos
Munoz-Yague/Eurelios). Environmental Images: pages 5 bottom (Rob
Visser), 26 (Martyn Bond), 28 (Robert Brook). Ecoscene: pages 10 (Kay
Hart), 11 top (Jim Winkley), 15 (Miessler), 19 bottom (Chris Knapton), 21
left and right, 27 top (Glover), 29 top (Angela Hampton). e.t. archive:
page 13 (National Gallery, London). Panos Pictures: page 23 (Jeremy
Homer), 25 top (Fred Hoogervorst), 25 bottom (Sean Sprague), 29 (J.
Holmes).
Artwork: Raymond Turvey

Franklin Wattts is a division of Hachette Children's Books,
an Hachette Livre UK company.

Note to parents and teachers: Every
effort has been made by the publisher to
ensure that websites listed are suitable for
children, that they are of the highest
educational value, and that they contain
no inappropriate or offensive material.
However, because of the nature of the
Internet, it is impossible to guarantee that
the contents of these sites will not be
altered. We strongly advise that Internet
access is supervised by a responsible adult.

CONTENTS

CLIMATE CHANGES

Our climate seems to be in the news all the time. Every day, we read about storms, droughts and heat waves. The Earth is getting warmer. Scientists call this global warming.

People sunbathe in Spain. Climate change is making the world warmer.

Why is it happening?

In the past, the world's climate has often changed naturally. It has been warmer than today, and colder. Now it is getting warmer. But scientists think that, this time, people are causing this. We are burning fuels such as coal, oil and natural gas. These make gases that help cause global warming.

*This **reservoir** is nearly empty. It has not rained here for a long time.*

What next?

No one knows exactly how our climate will change. Some places may get less rain and may get much hotter. Ice all over the world may melt, but some places may get colder. There may be more unusual **weather**. All these changes will affect the world we live in.

A flood from the Mississippi River in the USA. Climate change makes floods like these more likely.

5

WHAT IS CLIMATE?

Climate is the kind of weather a place usually gets over a long time. For example, in Europe we have warm summers and cold winters. Our weather can change each day, but the climate stays the same.

Different climates

The areas around the middle of the Earth have a climate that is warm all year. This is a tropical climate. The places further north and south have temperate climates, with cold winters and warm summers. Near the North and South poles, it is cold all year.

Polar bears live in the Arctic, where it is always cold.

CLIMATES

- Polar
- Temperate
- Desert
- Tropical
- Equatorial

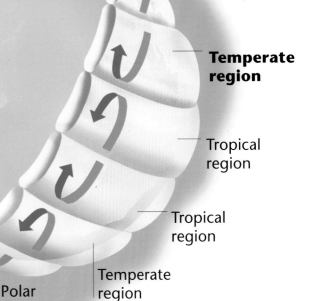

HOW THE SUN'S RAYS WARM THE EARTH

The Sun

At the **Equator**, the Sun's heat is not spread out.

Polar region

Temperate region

The Sun's rays

Tropical region

Away from the Equator, the Sun's heat spreads over a wider area.

Tropical region

Temperate region

Polar region

Eco Thought

Each day, the Sun sends us as much energy as 200 million power stations.

The Sun heats the Earth unevenly. This causes winds, which carry warmth, cold and rain across the Earth's surface.

The Sun and climate

In the **tropics**, the Sun sends heat straight down to the Earth, so these places have hot climates. Near the poles, the Sun is lower in the sky. Its rays have to travel further to reach the Earth. They hit the ground at an angle, so the heat is spread out more. The climate is colder.

When the Sun is low in the sky, less heat reaches Earth.

7

OCEANS

Climate is very complicated. Lots of things can affect climate. These include the oceans, which cover around two thirds of the Earth's surface.

Most the Earth's surface is covered by the sea.

Oceans and climates

In the tropics, the Sun warms the surface of the oceans. This warm water is lighter, and rises. In the far north and south, the water is colder. It is heavier, and sinks. All this makes the water move. We call these movements ocean **currents**.

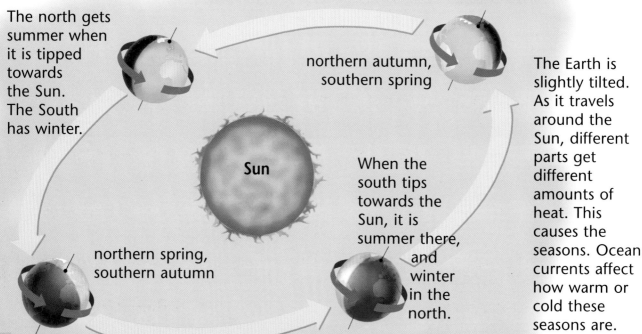

The north gets summer when it is tipped towards the Sun. The South has winter.

northern autumn, southern spring

Sun

When the south tips towards the Sun, it is summer there, and winter in the north.

northern spring, southern autumn

The Earth is slightly tilted. As it travels around the Sun, different parts get different amounts of heat. This causes the seasons. Ocean currents affect how warm or cold these seasons are.

Currents

Currents can warm or cool the air above the sea. The Gulf Stream is a warm current. It flows along the east coast of North America to north-western Europe, and stops

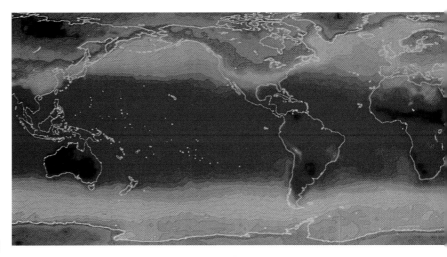

On this map, the warmest water is red, and the coldest is blue.

our winters from getting too cold. A cold current normally flows north along the coast of South America. Every few years, it turns into a warm current, and flows the other way. When this happens, it is called 'El Niño', or 'The Child'. It causes rain in some places, and droughts in others.

Bangladesh often has floods. Its hot and wet climate is affected by changes in sea currents.

Eco Thought

An El Niño in 1997 had a stronger effect that any other for 100 years. It caused droughts in Australia and Indonesia, and floods in Japan and North America.

9

CLIMATE CLUES

People have been writing about the climate for hundreds of years. Because of this, we know what the weather was like in the past. This is one way we can tell that today's climate is changing.

Clues from ice

Glaciers are masses of ice in high mountains and at the North and South poles. The ice in these may be thousands of years old. Scientists study air trapped inside it to learn about what the Earth's climate was like when the glacier formed.

There are glaciers in Alaska that are thousands of years old.

Tree records

Every year, a tree grows a new ring of wood inside its trunk. These are widest when the weather is warm and wet. Some trees live for hundreds of years, and have hundreds of rings. These can show us how the climate has changed.

Records show spring flowers bloom earlier now, because the climate is warmer.

In this slice of a tree trunk we can see rings that show how old the tree was when it was cut.

On the Ground

Some trees in the USA are over 5,000 years old. Scientists study these to learn about climates in the past.

Try this

Count the rings on a tree stump. How old was the tree? Can you see wide and narrow rings?

NATURAL CHANGES

The climate can change naturally.
Erupting volcanoes, or changes in the
Sun can cause this.

Volcanic dust

When a **volcano** erupts, it throws
tonnes of dust and acid into the air.
These can stop some of the Sun's
heat from reaching the Earth.

Activity of the Sun

Sometimes the Sun gives out more
heat than at other times. When it
gives out less heat, the climate of
the Earth is cooler.

On the Ground

In the 1600s, the climate
was colder than today.
The River Thames in
London often froze
in winter.

*Close-up of the
surface of the
Sun. When it
changes, so
can the
Earth.*

Past climates

The dinosaurs lived over 65 million years ago. Climates then were warmer. There were forests near the South Pole, where nothing grows now. In the last million years, there have been times when the climate has been very cold. We call these **Ice Ages**.

In the 1600s, the climate in Europe was so cold that we call this time the Little Ice Age.

Eco Thought

In the 1930s, a **drought** made the soil in part of the USA so dry that people called the area the Dust Bowl.

This desert in Africa was a swamp millions of years ago. We can see a dinosaur's footprint.

A GREENHOUSE

The glass in a greenhouse traps the Sun's heat and keeps the greenhouse warm. Some gases around the Earth do this, too. These are greenhouse gases.

Clouds float high in the air above the Earth. This air holds the Sun's heat close to the Earth.

Global warming

We need greenhouse gases to keep the Earth warm. But there is much more greenhouse gas in our **atmosphere** than before. This is like making the glass in a greenhouse thicker, so it traps more heat. Most scientists think this is the main reason why the Earth is getting warmer.

Eco Thought

Carbon dioxide is a greenhouse gas. There is nearly a third more in the air now than 200 years ago.

Greenhouse gases

Greenhouse gases are increasing as people burn more **fossil fuels** (coal, oil and gas). When we burn these, carbon dioxide forms. This is a major greenhouse gas. As we burn more fossil fuels, more carbon dioxide forms.

The glass in a greenhouse traps heat from the Sun. It keeps plants warm, even in cold weather.

Energy from the Sun reaches the Earth.

Some bounces back into space.

HOW THE EARTH'S ATMOSPHERE ACTS LIKE A GREENHOUSE

Some energy passes through the atmosphere. It changes into heat.

The atmosphere traps this heat, so the Earth warms up.

Try this

Check the temperature in a greenhouse in the early morning. Check again in the middle of the day. See how warm it can get.

GETTING WARMER

We know the Earth is getting warmer because people have kept records for 150 years.

Keeping track

Today, we have weather stations, ships and satellites to check what is happening to our climate. These collect information about air and sea temperatures, the wind and the clouds. They put this into computers, to work out how the climate will change. We know the climate has never changed as fast as it is doing today.

As the Earth gets warmer, more rivers will dry out, like this one in Africa.

A scientist checks the amount of carbon dioxide in the atmosphere. She can compare it with the amount in the past.

Warmer nights

Greenhouse gases are good at trapping heat at night, so nights are getting warmer faster than days. In many places, there used to be more frosts at night than there are now. Also, spring and autumn climates are getting more like each other.

A scientist uses a computer to study the weather all over the world.

On the Ground

Sound travels faster through warmer water. Scientists are sending sounds through the Indian Ocean, to see if the water there is getting warmer.

GREENHOUSE GASES

Some greenhouse gases are produced naturally. Others are made by factories, cars and aircraft.

Carbon dioxide

Most living things produce the gas carbon dioxide when they breathe. Wood, oil, gas and coal contain the chemical carbon. When factories and **vehicles** burn these fuels, they also give off carbon dioxide. Every year, six billion tonnes of carbon dioxide gets into the atmosphere.

When power stations like this burn coal, they produce greenhouse gases.

There are more and more people on Earth, producing more and more carbon dioxide.

Try this

Use weather reports in newspapers or on the radio, and record the weather. How does it change during the week?

Other gases

Methane is a greenhouse gas. Tiny living things called bacteria produce it. It is found in marshy places, sewage plants, and by animals. Nitrous oxide is another gas produced by **fertilizers** and burning some fuels. **HFCs** are gases that were once used in fridges. They are 3,000 times stronger than carbon dioxide.

Eco Thought

Methane forms in cows' stomachs. A cow belches 500 litres of it every day.

When car engines burn petrol, they give off greenhouse gases.

19

THE RISING SEA

Global warming is making sea levels rise. Scientists think they will rise by 75 centimetres in the next 50 years.

As sea levels rise, waves may get bigger.

Melting ice

Seas are rising because the water is getting warmer. Warm water takes up more space than cold water. Also, glaciers on mountains, and ice at the poles is melting, adding water to the sea.

Islands under threat

Many people live on small islands and on low-lying land near the sea. These people's homes will be flooded as sea levels rise. Some islands may vanish. So may cities such as Venice, Italy and Miami, USA.

Stormy weather

Hurricanes are storms that form over warm seas. They get their energy from the warm water. As seas get warmer, there may be more hurricanes, and more violent ones.

The picture on the left was taken in 1990. It shows a beach on an island in the Indian Ocean. The picture on the right was taken in 1995. The beach has washed away.

MORE DESERT

Deserts are getting bigger because of global warming. Soon, places that were once good farms may become desert.

Droughts and forest fires

The Sahel is an area south of the Sahara Desert in Africa. It is much drier there than it was 50 years ago. There are more droughts. Crops often fail to grow, so many people do not have enough food. The Mediterranean region is north of the Sahara desert. Here, the summers are getting hotter and drier, causing droughts and forest fires.

Cattle used to drink at this water hole in the Sahel. But now it is dry.

Less farmland

Global warming means farming will change. For example, sunflowers and maize will grow further north than they do now. But, in the end, there will be less land where crops can grow.

One day, this farmland in the USA may be too dry for crops.

Sunflowers can now grow in places that were once too cool for them.

23

LOTS OF PESTS

As the climate gets warmer, new animals might move into places where they did not live before. These can affect our crops and our health.

This scientist is studying the diseases insects can bring to wheat plants.

Carrying disease

Many mosquitoes spread dangerous diseases. Some carry the tiny creatures that cause a disease called **malaria**. Others carry germs that cause yellow fever and dengue fever. As the climate gets warmer, these mosquitoes may start to live in places that are too cold for them now.

Eco Thought
Many traditional healers use tropical plants to cure diseases.

This farmer in Kenya is spraying his cattle. It will protect them from insects that carry disease.

Pests on the move

Mosquitoes are moving to places that used to be too cool for them. There are mosquitoes in the Mediterranean, in Florida and the mountain areas of Africa that carry the disease malaria. Yellow fever has reached Ethiopia, Africa. Dengue fever has reached Texas, USA. Other insect pests may spread, too, as the climate gets warmer. These might include locusts, which destroy crops.

A swarm of locusts attacks crops in Africa. Climate change may mean they spread further.

On The Ground

Caterpillars called budworms are attacking **conifer** trees in Alaska. Warmer summers may be helping these insects to breed more often.

NEW FUELS

Fossil fuels were made from the remains of plants and animals, millions of years ago. They contain carbon. Burning them sends carbon dioxide into the air.

*These are **solar panels**. They trap the Sun's energy, and turn it into electricity.*

Making electricity

We can produce less carbon dioxide if we burn less fossil fuel. Instead, we can make electricity from the wind, or running water, or from the Sun. These are sources of energy that do not run out. We call them **renewable sources**.

Eco Thought

All the fridges in the USA together make as much electricity as 20 power stations.

These big propellors are called turbines. As the wind turns them, they can create electricity.

Wind and waste

When we burn fossil fuels we add carbon dioxide to the air. If we use other fuels we can reduce this. We can build more wind turbines to make electricity. We can use also use waste from rotted plants. As the waste rots it makes a gas called **biogas** that can be used for cooking and heating.

Some people use cow dung as fuel. This is makes less carbon dioxide than fossil fuels.

On the Ground
Biogas can be made from cow dung. Six cows can make enough gas for a whole family.

27

WHAT CAN WE DO?

There are many ways we can help stop the climate from changing too much. Schools and families can help. We must all work together.

Save energy

If we save energy, we can burn less fossil fuels. We can turn heating down. We can turn lights off in empty rooms. We can use light bulbs that do not use much energy. There are also new cars and power stations that use less fuel.

A factory once stood on this land. Now trees are growing here.

Eco Thought
A quarter of all the carbon dioxide made comes from homes.

A lot of fuel is used to make glass, tins and aluminium containers. If we recycle these, we save energy.

Planting trees

Trees give out carbon dioxide, but they take in much more. If we burn wood from trees that we have planted specially for firewood, we save forests. We can also plant new trees. These will absorb carbon dioxide.

Cycling or walking saves using cars and the fuel they burn.

FACT FILE

Using less energy

If one per cent of homes in the USA replaced their light bulbs with energy-saving lights, this is what they would save in a year: $800 million in electricity costs; two and a half billion kg of coal; eight billion kg of carbon dioxide and other polluting gases. It would save enough energy to light 300,000 homes.

Forest fires

There is more danger now of forest fires in Yellowstone National Park in the USA. Summers are getting higher and droughts are lasting longer.

Melting ice

Siberia, in Russia, is warming up. Once the ground was frozen all the time. Now it is soggy in some areas. Buildings there are tipping over.

Rats

In 1994 in India, there were record high temperatures and heavy monsoon rains. This helped rats to breed. They spread a deadly disease called bubonic **plague**.

Too hot!

There was a heat wave in Europe in the summer of 2003. Thousands of people died from heart and breathing problems, because of the heat.

Websites

www.wattwatchers.org

www.yptenc.org.uk

www.nationalgeographic.org/kids

www.oneworld.net/penguin

GLOSSARY

Atmosphere The layer of gases around the Earth.

Biogas A gas that is given off by dead plants or animals as they rot.

Conifers Type of trees, such as fir and pine, which keep their leaves all year round.

Current A flow of water or air.

Drought A long period without rain.

Equator An imaginary line around the middle of the Earth.

Fertilizers Substances added to the soil to help crops grow.

Fossil fuels Fuels formed from plants and animals that died millions of years ago.

Glacier A slow-moving mass of ice that travels down mountain valleys.

HFCs Hydrofluorocarbons -used to cool fridges.

Hurricane Powerful tropical storms in America. In other parts of the world they are called typhoons or cyclones.

Ice Age A period of cold, which can last for thousands of years.

Malaria A disease caused by tiny living things that are carried by a certain kind of mosquito.

Methane A kind of gas that can be burned. Burning it gives off carbon dioxide.

Plague Another name for bubonic plague, but it can also mean large numbers of a pest.

Polar region The areas close to the North and South Poles

Renewable sources Energy from sources that do not run out, such as from the wind or sun.

Reservoir A lake made for storing water.

Solar panel A flat panel used to collect energy from the Sun. Some collect heat to warm water, others change the Sun's energy into electricity.

Temperate region A part of the world that has warm summers and colder winters.

Tropics Hot, wet parts of the world, near the Equator.

Vehicle Cars, buses or any other machine for carrying things or people.

Volcano A hole in the outer crust of the Earth. Hot rocks and gas may escape through it onto the Earth's surface.

Weather Warmth in the air, rain, sunshine, wind and anything else that affects the air around us in a place at any one time.

INDEX